MILITARY JOBS

NAVY SEALS

▷ What It Takes to Join the Elite

ALEXANDER STILWELL

Cavendish
Square

New York

Published in 2015 by Cavendish Square Publishing, LLC
243 5th Avenue, Suite 136, New York, NY 10016

© 2015 Brown Bear Books Ltd

First edition

Website: cavendishsq.com

This publication represents the opinions and views of the author based on his or her personal experiences, knowledge, and research. The information in this book serves as a general guide only. The author and publisher have used their best efforts in preparing this book and disclaim liability rising directly or indirectly from the use and application of this book.

CPSIA compliance information: Batch #WW15CSQ.

All websites were available and accurate when this book was sent to press.

Library of Congress Cataloging-in-Publication Data

Stillwell, Alexander.
Navy SEALs: What it Takes to Join the Elite / Alexander Stillwell.
    pages cm. — (Military jobs)
 Includes index.
 ISBN 978-1-50260-226-8 (hardcover) ISBN 978-1-50260-227-5 (ebook)
1. United States. Navy. SEALs—Juvenile literature. 2. United States. Navy. SEALs—Vocational guidance—Juvenile literature. I. Title.

 VG87.S72 2015
 359.9'84—dc23

                    2014022797

For Brown Bear Books Ltd:
Editorial Director: Lindsey Lowe
Managing Editor: Tim Cooke
Children's Publisher: Anne O'Daly
Design Manager: Keith Davis
Designer: Lynne Lennon
Picture Manager: Sophie Mortimer

Picture Credits:
T=Top, C=Center, B=Bottom, L=Left, R=Right

Front Cover : FC All images Library of Congress
All images © Library of Congress, except; 10, © Bettmann/Corbis; 30, © Shutterstock.

Manufactured in the United States of America

CONTENTS

INTRODUCTION

The Sea, Air, Land (SEAL) teams are the elite special forces of the U.S. Navy. They are trained to be ready to react to military situations at short notice, anywhere in the world—even miles from the ocean.

There are about 2,700 SEALs at any time, so this is a small and exclusive force. The men who get to join have to pass a series of physical and mental tests to show they have got what it takes. Once they qualify as SEALs, they undergo constant training to prepare them for action in any situation. They learn to go into action by sea or by air, to survive in extreme conditions, and to operate in small teams.

The SEALs are at home in or on the water. They are also secretive about who they are and what they do. The first time most people even heard of the SEALs was in 2011. SEAL Team Six launched a daring nighttime helicopter assault on a house in Pakistan. They killed al-Qaeda terrorist leader Osama bin Laden in a firefight.

A four-man SEAL team practice clearing and securing a house during a training exercise.

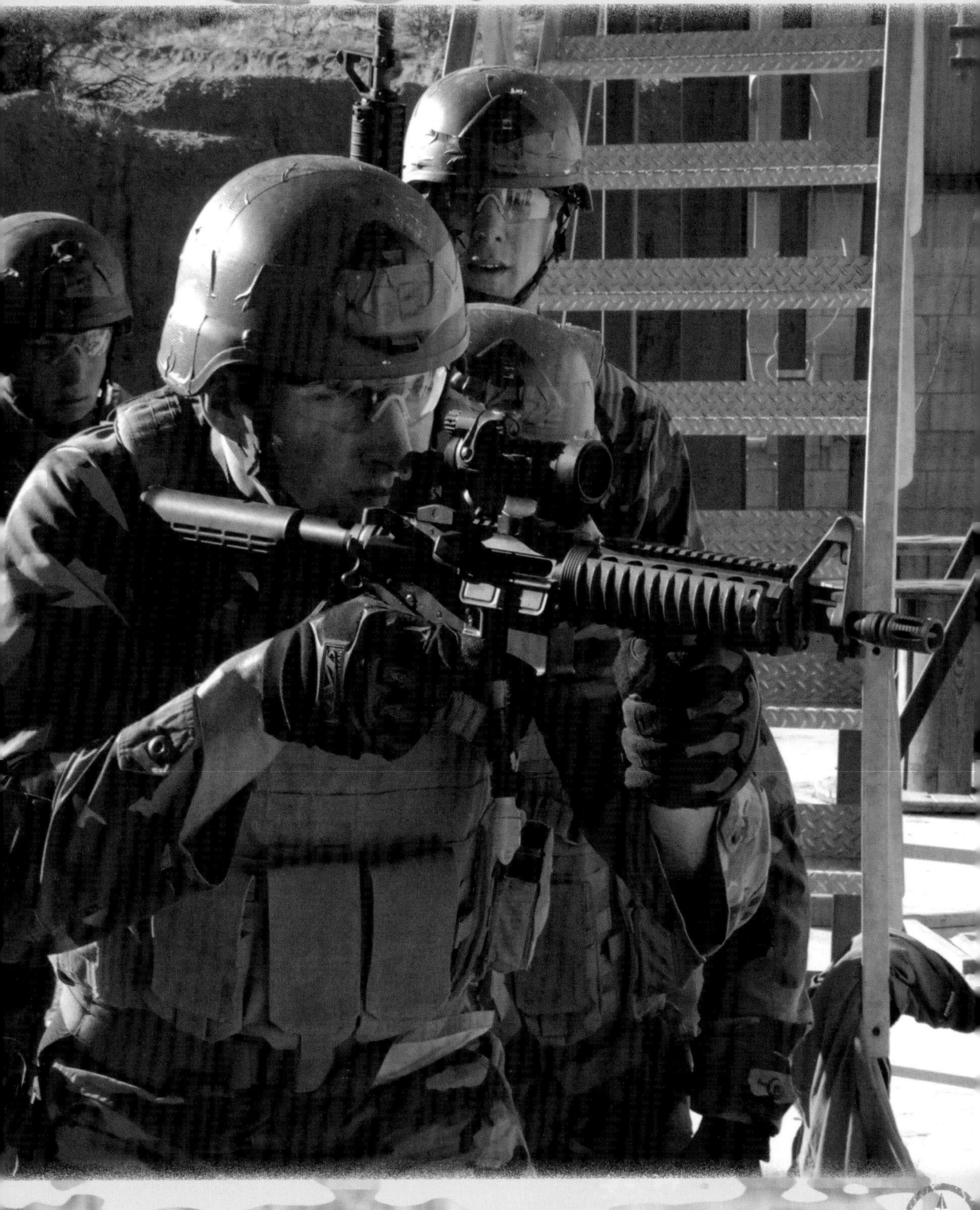

▶▶ HISTORY

The SEAL teams are based on U.S. Navy swimmer units that were used in World War II (1939–1945). In Europe and the Pacific, these divers swam ashore secretly to gather information about the enemy and to destroy obstacles for a following landing.

In 1962 U.S. forces were becoming involved in the war in Vietnam. President John F. Kennedy ordered the creation of two small elite teams to carry out unconventional maritime warfare. In Vietnam, these SEAL teams carried out successful operations against the enemy Viet Cong. They often moved deep inland after swimming ashore from submarines. They used boats to patrol Vietnam's many rivers. Their missions included rescuing U.S. prisoners of war.

◀◀ With their faces camouflaged, SEALs creep through the jungle on a mission in Vietnam.

President John F. Kennedy talks to combat divers from the new elite teams he created in 1962.

Since Vietnam, more SEAL teams have been created. There were some failures in the 1980s, when missions went wrong in Iran and Grenada, but they kept learning.

Improved Coordination

U.S. Special Operations Command (USSOCOM) was created to coordinate all the U.S. special forces. The SEALs report to Naval Special Warfare Command (NSW). NSW incorporates eight SEAL teams, one SEAL Delivery Vehicle (SDV) team, and three Special Boat Teams (SBT).

More recently, the role of the Navy SEALs has expanded to include anti-terrorism operations around the world.

EYEWITNESS

"We keep our units small and separate from large force operations. We have a niche here to be very good in units of often less than eight men."

—SEAL Team Commander

WHAT IT TAKES

To become a SEAL, you have to meet high physical and mental standards before you even start training. Special forces operate in some of the most challenging environments in the world and in situations that require physical stamina and quick thinking.

 SEAL instructors watch recruits doing push-ups as part of their physical tests.

"Cross-training such as cycling, rowing, and hiking is useful to rehabilitate an injury, to add variety, or to supplement your basic training."

—SEAL Physical Training Guide

To become a SEAL, a recruit has to be in the U.S. Navy, which means that he has already met certain standards of fitness and mental ability. But there are more tests to come. They include a series of medical screenings and various aptitude tests.

Physical Tests

For many candidates the biggest challenge is the physical tests (PST). They follow a training schedule to get ready to tackle the physical assessment and to prepare for Basic Underwater Demolition (BUD/S) training.

▶▶ Recruits are timed on a demanding assault course.

PHYSICAL TESTS
(PST AND PREPARATION COURSE)

The first thing a SEAL recruit has to prove is that he's physically fit. SEALs need to be able to operate effectively in extreme conditions on very little sleep, so it's important that their bodies are in good shape.

A recuit has to be able to do at least forty-two push-ups.

Physical fitness is measured in a series of Physical Tests (PST). Recruits are expected to achieve minimum scores. There are also optimum scores.

Recruits also take the Armed Services Vocational Aptitude Battery (ASVAB) and Armed Forces Qualification Test (AFQT). These tests cover

TEST	MINIMUM	COMPETITIVE
Swim 500 yards	12 mins 30 secs	10 mins 30 secs
Push-ups	42	79
Curl-ups	50	79
Pull-ups	6	11
Run 1.5 miles	11 mins	10 mins 20 secs

EYEWITNESS

"Your strength training should develop the necessary muscular strength for maximum pull-ups, push-ups, and sit-ups, as they are necessary for success at BUD/S."
—Jeff Krause, former SEAL

▷▷ **Recruits climb up and down either side of a tall wall with few handholds as part of a training assault course.**

a range of areas, including math knowledge, general science, assembling objects, and verbal expression. The minimum score is 35, but candidates who go on to do well at SEAL training have test scores of about 78 or higher.

Mental Toughness

To be a SEAL takes great mental control. Candidates are tested to find out how well they control their emotions, how they react to challenges, and how they relate to other people in pressure situations. SEALs have to think clearly and positively, even when facing great challenges.

►► BASIC UNDERWATER DEMOLITION

Once a recruit has passed the basic SEAL qualifications, the next step is Basic Underwater Demolition training (BUD/S) at the Naval Special Warfare Training Center in Coronado, CA.

▽ **Exhausted candidates crawl at the edge of the ocean during the notorious Hell Week.**

BUD/S begins with a five-week preparatory "warm up" course. After that, training is broken into three phases ... for recruits who make the grade:

▲ **Instructors in SCUBA gear watch recruits in an exercise in the pool.**

Phase 1: Physical conditioning
    – 8 weeks
Phase 2: Diving – 8 weeks
Phase 3: Land Warfare – 9 weeks

Phase 1

Only the best candidates make it through Phase 1, Physical Conditioning. This includes the notorious "Hell Week." The candidates are put through physical and mental training that gets tougher and tougher. They also learn water-based skills,

including swimming with fins and handling small boats. Each candidate is timed on a four-mile (6.4-km) run, an obstacle course, and a two-mile (3.20km) swim.

IN ACTION

There's a good reason why it is so tough to join the SEALs. On a special forces operation, sleep is rare and men operate at the limits of exhaustion. SEAL instructors have to be sure that a candidate will remain emotionally stable and make good decisions, even when they are worn out.

≫BUD/S: LAND AND SEA

If a candidate gets through the first phase of BUD/S, they start learning technical skills. These skills make a SEAL effective in the water or on land.

Crawling through pipes is just one part of the physical training.

Candidates who come through Phase 1 of training have proved they have the physical ability to be a SEAL.

Phase 2: Diving

While the physical training becomes even more demanding, Phase 2 includes more training about combat diving, which is the core of SEAL training. Candidates are put in the most stressful underwater situations so that they learn how to get out of emergencies themselves and also how to help their buddies. Instructors pull off the candidates' face masks or interfere with their equipment in order to test how each candidate will react to the situation.

Phase 3: Land Warfare

In the final phase of BUD/S, the SEALs come out of the water. They learn all the skills that they will need for operations on land, including weapons skills, navigation, rappelling, and demolitions. They also learn small-unit tactics and patrolling techniques.

EYEWITNESS

"Cold and wet is a tradition with the winter classes. It is inevitable. There is no way to avoid it. You WILL be cold and wet during BUD/S training."

—Jeff Krause

SEAL recruits paddle rubber boats out into the surf as part of a training exercise.

>> HELL WEEK

Hell Week is five-and-a-half days of extreme training. SEAL trainers set a series of demanding tests. Anything can happen—and the exhausted candidates will get only four hours' sleep during this time.

 Candidates test their strength and endurance by carrying logs weighing 150 lb (68 kg).

Hell Week may start with a bang as screaming instructors burst into a room firing machine gun blanks and ordering the candidates to crawl to the beach. From now on the recruits are under constant pressure.

 Instructors remind the recruits that they can give up at any time— and most do.

EYEWITNESS

"*This is a week during which the instructors are given carte blanche to deviate from the schedule as necessary to assure total demoralization of the class. This is a week when the majority of the class will quit or be forced out of training due to injuries.*"

—**Jeff Krause, former SEAL**

They perform punishing physical exercises. They face danger, such as landing on rocks from rubber craft in high waves. They are cold and wet all the time. In the water, they suffer uncontrollable shivers.

True Determination

As the candidates crawl through mud or sand, or lie on the beach waiting for the tide to break over their faces, they are tempted to give up and get a warm blanket. Only mental determination keeps the best of them going.

>> UNDERWATER TRAINING

SEALs, as their name suggests, are mainly trained to operate on, under, near, or from water. Their training makes sure that they are completely confident in any aquatic environment.

The BUD/S course includes what instructors call "drown-proofing." This consists of swimming three laps across the pool. On the first, recruits' hands are tied behind their back. On the second, their feet are tied together. On the third lap, both hands and feet are tied together. Recruits also learn to "bob." They must remain submerged, coming up only for a gulp of air before submerging again. If they show any signs of panic, they are thrown off the course. SEALs have to be completely at home underwater.

>> **A SEAL recruit masters breathing with SCUBA gear; SEALs have to be able to react calmly if anything goes wrong with their air supply.**

Combat Diving

The recruits start using SCUBA
(self-contained underwater
breathing apparatus) equipment
in the pool. They become familiar
with SCUBA gear. They are
made to perform detailed tasks
underwater, such as tying knots.

Outside the pool, recruits make
long-distance underwater dives.
This is important as SEALs have to
be able to swim ashore from boats
or submarines. All candidates
have to be able to swim at least
5.5 miles (9 km) in the ocean.

The first steps of SCUBA training
take place in the pool, where
recruits can be observed easily.

EYEWITNESS

"Scuba training consists of two
types—open circuit (compressed
air) and closed circuit (100 percent
oxygen). This is considered by many
to be the SEALs' raison d'être, and
accordingly lasts eight weeks."

—*U.S. Navy SEALs*, Osprey
Elite

 # INSERTION

U.S. Navy SEALs learn a wide range of techniques for getting in and out of the operational area. When SEALs are delivered to an operation by sea, it's important that they maintain secrecy.

The most essential element of many SEAL operations is suprise. The U.S. Navy uses water or air insertion to get SEALs into position without being spotted by the enemy.

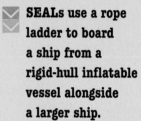 SEALs use a rope ladder to board a ship from a rigid-hull inflatable vessel alongside a larger ship.

By Water

SEALs are used to arriving for missions by water. Often they are delivered by a Navy ship or a submarine.

They go ashore either by using small rubber craft or by swimming long distances. By using the SEAL Delivery Vehicle (SDV), SEALs can be dropped off from a submarine without the submarine even having to surface. The SDV is like a small

 SEALS with masks and snorkels train in techniques for swimming ashore.

submersible, which takes the SEAL team into the shallows.

On the Beach

The SEALs' preferred time to come ashore is at night. They crawl through the surf onto the beach. They have goggles for nighttime vision. Their weapons and ammunition are waterproof, so they are ready to fire as soon as the SEALs hit land. They carry other equipment in waterproof cases, such as laser target finders, and unpack it when they reach land.

EYEWITNESS

"The SDV Mk VIII is one of the more interesting and secretive vehicles of the U.S. Naval special forces, and it is used to make sub-surface insertions."

—Encyclopedia of the World's Special Forces

AIR INSERTION

As well as by water, SEALs often go into missions by air. They parachute onto land or into water, drop from helicopters into the sea, or are lowered by ropes to the ground or the deck of a ship.

SEALs practice a parachute jump from a transport airplane during an exercise.

In a standard air delivery, a small rubber raiding craft is dropped from a low-flying airplane or helicopter into the ocean. The SEALs jump after it and use it to get ashore. If SEALs jump from a greater height, they use parachutes. They strap their swimming fins to their legs and put them on when they are in the water.

Rope Tricks

One of the most effective SEAL delivery techniques is Special Purpose Insertion and Extraction (SPIE). SEALs use harness and special attachments to hook themselves onto a rope lowered from a helicopter. Once all the SEALs are attached, they are lowered to the ground or lifted off it. The SPIE system is also adapted for use at sea.

The use of SPIE allows SEALs to carry specially trained dogs. These dogs can track personnel or detect bombs.

IN ACTION

The use of aircraft allows SEALs to get where they need to be quickly. In order to avoid detection, SEALs often use high-altitude, low-opening (HALO) jumps. They jump out of aircraft high above enemy radar but only open their parachutes when they are close to the ground.

23

COLD WEATHER SURVIVAL

As part of Seal Qualification Training (SQT), the SEALs spend four weeks at Kodiak in Alaska. The priority is survival so the SEALs are taught the basics for keeping warm. That means knowing how to build a shelter and light a fire.

The SEALs also learn how to navigate and how to locate and catch fish and other food in freezing, snow-covered areas. Navigation can be difficult when everything is covered in snow and looks the same. SEALs also learn how to move through snow, whether using snowshoes or skis, while carrying a weapon and all their equipment. They learn to survive using their basic kit, in case they have to drop their main equipment in an emergency.

Survial Skills

To test their survival ability, recruits are led on to the ice so that they fall through and spend five minutes

Even a small tent can make the difference between life and death.

in near-freezing water. They have to get out, put up their tents, and get a fire going to prevent hypothermia. Seconds count.

SEAL recruits emerge from icy water. The immersion test is designed to push their bodies and minds to the limit.

Fighting the Cold

Survival requires mental resilience. Cold reduces energy levels and the will to take action to ensure survival. Once these skills are mastered and the SEAL knows what he is up against, he will be much more confident and effective in an extreme cold operational environment.

EYEWITNESS

"We try to educate students on being smart about aligning their survival priorities. For Alaska, the most important priority is shelter; having the ability to get out of the elements and build a fire."

—SEAL Trainer, Kodiak

HOT WEATHER SURVIVAL

Many SEAL operations take place in tropical or desert conditions. These environments can be just as physically demanding as extreme cold, so U.S. Navy SEALs need to be able to withstand the heat.

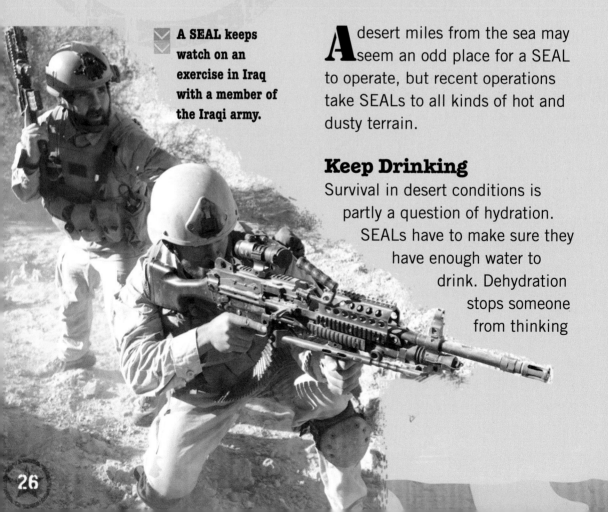

A SEAL keeps watch on an exercise in Iraq with a member of the Iraqi army.

A desert miles from the sea may seem an odd place for a SEAL to operate, but recent operations take SEALs to all kinds of hot and dusty terrain.

Keep Drinking

Survival in desert conditions is partly a question of hydration. SEALs have to make sure they have enough water to drink. Dehydration stops someone from thinking clearly, so it can endanger a whole mission. Proper headgear helps to avoid sunstroke.

Fighting Grit

One of the biggest dangers in desert conditions is dust or sand. It gets into weapons and stops them from firing. The best way to prevent this is to carry out constant careful cleaning. SEALs are trained to maintain their weapons to the highest possible level. They know that their lives might depend on a gun firing correctly.

IN ACTION

The SEALs ability to act in hot, dry, dusty conditions has been tested in major campaigns since 2000 in Afghanistan and Iraq. Much of both countries is desert, where SEALs cover the empty landscape using vehicles like Humvees and Desert Patrol Vehicles.

 Rifles at the ready, SEALs patrol through a grove of trees on a dusty hilside in Afghanistan.

AMPHIBIOUS SKILLS

SEALs mainly operate in or near water.
Their water-based skills cover a broad range.
For deep-water work like defusing mines or bombs,
SEALs will normally carry SCUBA gear.

A submarine sails away having left
two **SEAL** divers in the ocean.

 A SEAL frogman leaves the water with his rifle ready to fire.

If the SEALs are operating nearer the surface or in an area such as a port, bubbles from the SCUBA might give away their position to the enemy.

EYEWITNESS

"We keep one foot in the water. That means if we must do inland operations it is because they are attached to a maritime reason."

—**SEAL team commander**

Steath Diving

For stealth missions, SEALs wear a Drager LAR oxygen rebreather designed for stealth diving. The rebreather prevents any air escaping from the mouthpiece by absorbing the carbon dioxide the diver breathes out. By using rebreathers, SEALs can emerge from the sea or a river in full camouflage kit and still achieve complete surprise.

 SNIPERS

Once a SEAL has completed all the phases of his training, he may be invited to sniper school. To be a sniper, you need to be a special breed of person. You need to have above average patience and determination and extraordinary marksmanship skills.

Even SEALs consider sniper training to be the toughest training course they have to go through—if they are lucky enough to have been selected to attend it. The course consists of three months of twelve-hour days, seven days per week.

A Mental Challenge

On this course it is not so much the physical challenge that is tested but the mental challenge. The snipers are taught how to spend hours crawling through undergrowth, through water, or over hot desert sand to get close enough to the target.

 Once in position, snipers can remain camouflaged and motionless for hours at a time.

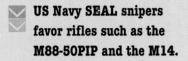

US Navy SEAL snipers favor rifles such as the M88-50PIP and the M14.

The modern sniper has to understand technology, including handheld computers and satellite systems. He also needs to be a master of stealth and concealment. Snipers have to infiltrate enemy areas and get within range of the target. They must also be able to get away without leaving a trace.

Two-Man Teams

Snipers often operate in a two-man team. One man is the marksman. The other is a spotter. As they wait in position—sometimes for many hours—the spotter keeps watch so the sniper does not break his concentration.

EYEWITNESS

"It was my duty to shoot the enemy, and I don't regret it. My regrets are for the people I couldn't save: Marines, soldiers, buddies. The worst moments of my life have come as a SEAL. But I can stand before God with a clear conscience about doing my job."

—Chris Kyle, SEAL Sniper

SEAL DELIVERY VEHICLE

The SEAL Delivery Vehicle (SDV) is used for underwater operations, saving the SEALs time in swimming to their targets. It is manned by a pilot and co-pilot who are often part of the six-man raiding team. The SDV can carry equipment and mines.

The Seal Delivery Vehicle (SDV) is a Mk VIII SDV minisub. It takes SEALs close to their targets. It has an electronic engine, so it does not make any noise or produce any bubbles that would give its position away. To operate in dark water or at nighttime, the SDV has a sonar device for navigation. It can carry four fully equipped SEALs, as well as heavy equipment such as mines. If the pilot and co-pilot are not part of the SEAL team, they are part of the specialized

 Members of SEAL Deilvery Vehicle Team 2 use a special hatch to leave a submarine underwater.

Seal Delivery Vehicle Team. The submersible is not enclosed, so the crew and passengers have to wear SCUBA gear.

 Pilots prepare to dock an SDV in a dry dock shelter on the deck of a submerged submarine.

Stealthy Exit

To carry an SDV, U.S. submarines are fitted with a dry-dock shelter. This is a tank on the deck that can be filled or emptied of water, so that the SEALs can launch the SDV without the submarine having to surface. SDVs are vital, because they mean that SEALs can operate from much longer range than if they had to swim to their targets.

EYEWITNESS

"For practice, we did race tracks. A race track was a clockwise or counter-clockwise lap around the sail of the sub as it moved along at slow speed. Newby [new] navigators often lost the sub and played catch up for hours."

—B.P Grogan, **SEAL Delivery Vehicle Team 2**, on learning to pilot a SDV.

OFFSHORE BOATS

Special Boat Teams (SBTs) are specially trained to work closely with SEALs. They use a range of boats to drop the Navy SEALs near their targets.

The Mark V Special Operations Craft has a top speed of about 75 miles per hour (120 km/h). It can get SEALs close to shore without being detected.

The U.S. Navy has three SBTs, which have a total of about 700 members. One of their key duties is to patrol the ocean just off the coast. If necessary, they can intercept or board hostile craft that are heading to or from land. For these operations, and for getting SEALs into action, the Boat Teams use a powerful Patrol Boat Coast (PBC). The PBC has

four diesel engines that generate speeds of up to 35 knots (40 miles per hour). They are heavily armed, with two 25mm autocannons, five .50 caliber machine guns, two grenade launchers, two machine guns, and six surface-to-air missiles (SAMs).

Mark V

The Mark V Special Operations Craft is used for operations closer to shore. It powers through the

water at over 65 knots (75 miles per hour) and carries both 7.62mm Gatling guns and .50 caliber machine guns. The craft has a low radar signature, and its V-shape design also helps its speed.

IN ACTION

Special Boat Teams are sometimes known as the "Brown Water Navy." The name comes from their time in Vietnam, when they patrolled the many rivers of the Mekong Delta. Today the SBTs still have boats for use on rivers rather than at sea.

Members of a SEAL team keep a low profile as they approach the shore in a fast F470 Combat Rubber Raiding Craft.

RAIDING AND RIVER CRAFT

One of the SEALs' most useful types of boat is the inflatable rubber raiding craft. These are highly adaptable and maneuverable. Their rubber hulls are strong but flexible, making them ideal for landing on rocky coasts as well as beaches.

Wearing reflector strips, recuits carry a rubber boat ashore during a nighttime drill.

Combat rubber raiding craft (CRRC) can be dropped by coastal patrol boats, which have a platform at the back for the purpose. For fast insertion, SEALs use the F470 Combat Rubber Raiding Craft. It has a powerful engine and can carry six SEAL raiders, together with its two-man crew.

River Craft

The Special Operations Craft–Riverine (SOC-R) is designed for fast insertion and extraction on or near rivers. It is powered by water jets, and its crew of four can deliver eight SEAL raiders.

 SEAL recruits make a hazardous landing on a rocky coast in heavy surf.

EYEWITNESS

"The SEALs rolled aboard their CRRCs and began unshipping the engines and securing their gear. The SEALS, black-faced, in black garb, aboard black CRRCs, were all but invisble on the black water."
—Keith Douglass, *SEAL Team Seven*

▶▶ HELICOPTERS

Like other special forces, the Navy SEALs often use helicopters to get to a mission—and to get away again. Helicopters are more adaptable than fixed-wing aircraft, because they can fly low and slowly, and can even hover in one place.

A SEAL drops straight into the ocean from an SH60 Seahawk helicopter flying low above the waves.

Because SEALs operate in six-man teams, they can be carried in combat helicopters such as the Black Hawk. These aircraft are gunships, with machine guns and rocket and missile launchers.

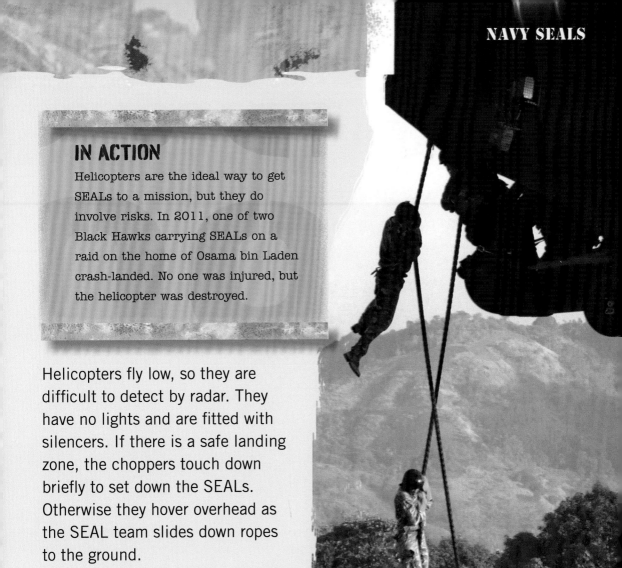

IN ACTION

Helicopters are the ideal way to get SEALs to a mission, but they do involve risks. In 2011, one of two Black Hawks carrying SEALs on a raid on the home of Osama bin Laden crash-landed. No one was injured, but the helicopter was destroyed.

Helicopters fly low, so they are difficult to detect by radar. They have no lights and are fitted with silencers. If there is a safe landing zone, the choppers touch down briefly to set down the SEALs. Otherwise they hover overhead as the SEAL team slides down ropes to the ground.

Tansport Helicopters

Transport helicopters such as the Chinook CH-47D can carry far more men and equipment. They are slow, however, and make an easy target for enemies on the ground. For that reason, they are not used often in hostile war zones.

 SEALs leave a helicopter by "fast-roping," or rappelling, down ropes.

▶▶ SEAL WEAPONS

SEALs are trained to use all sorts of weapons. Many of the men have a favorite type of gun. Usually a team will all use similar weapons, so they can share ammunition if they need to.

A SEAL going into action carries weapons such as hand grenades, which can be used to destroy obstacles such as doors or to clear rooms in house-to-house searches. He also carries a knife for hand-to-hand fighting. Most SEALs like to carry a pistol in a holster.

Rifle Power

The basic weapon for a SEAL is his rifle. It might be a sniper rifle, which is

◀◀ **This SEAL's M4 carbine is fitted with an M203 grenade launcher.**

◀◀ This M4A1
SOPMOD
carbine
has been
modified for
special forces
operations.

accurate over a long range. Or it might be a weapon like the M4A1 carbine, which is designed to be powerful. Some SEALs even use Russian-made AK47s. Their moving parts are so simple they are easy to maintain and rarely jam.

EYEWITNESS

"What does it take to make a Navy SEAL sniper? ... We seek out a special breed of man; a man who will wait hours and more for that perfect shot."

—Chris Hagerman, SEAL

KNIGHT'S ARMAMENT MK11 SNIPER WEAPON SYSTEM (SWS)

This rifle was developed especially according to specifications laid down by the U.S. Navy SEALs.

Caliber: 7.62mm (0.3in)
Weight: 15.3lbs (6.9kg)
Length: 45.5in (1,155mm)
Effective range: over 1,000 yards

M82A1 SPECIAL APPLICATION SCOPED RIFLE (SASR)

Navy SEALs use this rifle for heavy duty operations to take out vehicles or hit targets at extreme range.

Caliber: .50 BMG
Weight: 31.0lbs
Length: 48 or 57in
Effective range: 1,800m

MAERSK ALABAMA

When pirates seized the U.S. cargo ship MV *Maersk Alabama* off Somalia in April 2009 and took the crew hostage, snipers of the U.S. Naval Special Warfare Development Group (DEVGRU) were sent to East Africa. They are better known as SEAL Team Six.

 The pirates seized the *Maersk Alabama*. They aimed to force the ship's owners to pay a ransom.

The pirates were holding the captain of the ship, Richard Phillips, in a covered lifeboat that was being towed behind the *Maersk Alabama*.

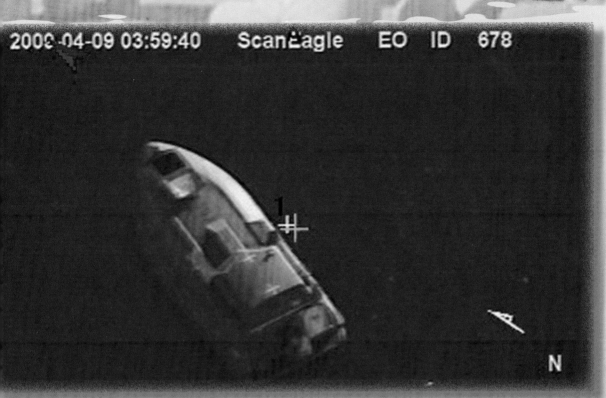

2009-04-09 03:59:40   ScanEagle   EO ID 678

1

N

U.S. Navy warships rushed to the scene and shadowed the ship. Meanwhile, the SEAL team flew in secretly and took up position on the destroyer USS *Bainbridge*.

Fatal Shots

The snipers could only see the pirates through small portholes. Both boats were moving. The SEALs waited for all three pirates to come into view, controlled their breathing, and squeezed their triggers. The three shots killed the three pirates with shots to the head. Phillips was rescued.

Three pirates took *Maersk Alabama*'s Captain Phillips hostage in a covered lifeboat, which was photographed by an unmanned U.S. drone.

EYEWITNESS

"Two of the captors poked their heads out of a rear hatch, exposing themselves to clear shots, and the third could be seen through a window... There were three shots, one each by three SEAL snipers."

—SEAL Team Commander

ABBOTTABAD 2011

Following the terrorist attacks in New York, Washington, and Pennsylvania on September 11, 2001, when nearly 3,000 people were killed, Osama bin Laden became the world's most wanted man.

Bin Laden led al-Qaeda, the terrorist group that launched the attacks. He just managed to get away when U.S. and NATO special forces invaded Afghanistan in 2001. The hunt went cold until intelligence agencies identified a messenger used by bin Laden. The CIA tracked him to a compound in Abbottabad in Pakistan. SEAL Team Six started practicing making a raid on a full-scale model of the house.

Night Raid

In the middle of the night on May 1, 2011, two Black Hawk MH-60 stealth helicopters took off from Afghanistan for Abbottabad. One helicopter crash-landed inside the compound. The other landed

 U.S. intelligence hunted Osama bin Laden for over a decade.

EYEWITNESS

"With security gates and walls up to 18 feet (5.5 m) tall, the residence of Osama bin Laden in Abbottabad was by far the most secure property in the area."

—News report

 President Barack Obama (second from left) and his senior colleagues watch the raid unfold.

outside, and the SEALs scaled the wall to enter the complex. The SEALs from both helicopters used explosives to blow their way into the house. They were soon involved in firefights with occupants of the house.

Mission Complete

The SEALs fought their way up to the third floor, where they located bin Laden and shot him dead. They destroyed the crashed helicopter before heading back to Bagram air base with bin Laden's body.

GLOSSARY

anti-terrorism Operations that are designed to discover and prevent planned terrorist attacks.

aptitude A natural ability to perform a certain type of task.

combat swimmer A soldier or sailor trained to swim into position ready to fight.

drone An unmanned aerial vehicle used for reconnaissance or to carry out bombing attacks.

frogman A swimmer equipped to operate freely underwater.

hostage Someone who is held captive and released in return for a payment of money.

inflatable A small vessel with a rubber hull filled with air.

insertion The act of delivering military personnel ready to begin a mission.

maritime Related to the sea.

navigation The act of finding out one's geographical location and planning a route.

pirate A person who attacks and robs ships at sea.

rappel To slide quickly down a rope.

rebreather An underwater breathing device that prevents gases being released into the water.

reconnaissance To use observation to find out about an enemy's positions.

SCUBA An abbreviation standing for Self-Contained Underwater Breathing Apparatus.

snorkel A breathing tube used by divers on the surface.

sonar A system that locates objects underwater by sending out sound waves.

spotter A person who helps a sniper identify a target.

submersible A small craft that can operate underwater.

unconventional Describes a type of warfare that uses ambush and secret attacks, rather than battles.

FURTHER INFORMATION

BOOKS

Besel, Jennifer M. *Navy SEALs.*
Elite Military Forces. Mankato, MN:
Capstone Press, 2011.

Cooke, Tim. *US Navy SEALs.*
Ultimate Special Forces. New York,
NY: PowerKids Press, 2013.

Gordon, Nick. *Navy SEALs.*
U.S. Military. Minneapolis, MN:
Bellwether Media, 2012.

Hamilton, John. *Navy SEALs.*
United States Armed Forces.
Minneapolis, MN: Abdo Group,
2011.

Payment, Simone. *Navy SEALs.*
Inside Special Operations.
New York, NY: Rosen Central, 2009.

Person, Stephen. *Navy SEAL Team
Six in Action.* Special Ops II.
New York, NY: Bearport Publishing,
2013.

Yomtov, Nel. *Navy SEALs in Action.*
Special Ops. New York, NY:
Bearport Publishing, 2008.

WEBSITES

**www.sealswcc.com/seal-default.
html**
The official website of the Navy
SEALs, with videos and features.

**science.howstuffworks.com/navy-seal.
htm**
Pages on the SEALs from
Howstuffworks.com.

navyseals.com
Privately run site with resources
about Navy SEAL training and life.

**www.military.com/special-operations/
training-to-be-a-navy-seal.html**
Military.com site about training to
become a SEAL.

Publisher's note to educators and parents: Our editors have carefully reviewed these websites to ensure that they are suitable for students. Many websites change frequently, however, and we cannot guarantee that a site's future contents will continue to meet our high standards of quality and educational value. Be advised that students should be closely supervised whenever they access the Internet.

INDEX